New Mexico

Jill Wheeler

Visit us at
www.abdopublishing.com

Published by ABDO Publishing Company, 8000 West 78th Street, Suite 310, Edina, Minnesota 55439 USA. Copyright ©2010 by Abdo Consulting Group, Inc. International copyrights reserved in all countries. No part of this book may be reproduced in any form without written permission from the publisher. The Checkerboard Library™ is a trademark and logo of ABDO Publishing Company.

Printed in the United States.

Editor: John Hamilton
Graphic Design: Sue Hamilton
Cover Illustration: Neil Klinepier
Cover Photo: iStock Photo
Interior Photo Credits: AirPhoto/Jim Wark, Alamy, AP Images, Comstock, Corbis, David Olson, Elizabeth Frye Jeffress, Getty, Granger Collection, iStock Photo, Ken Lund, Library of Congress, Mile High Maps, Mountain High Maps, NASA, New Mexico State Parks, New Mexico State Records Center and Archives, New Mexico State University, North Wind Picture Archives, One Mile Up, Photo Researchers, US Air Force/Markus Maier/John Strong II/Tiffany Trojca, University of New Mexico, and the Valles Caldera National Preserve/Don Usner.
Statistics: State population statistics taken from 2008 U.S. Census Bureau estimates. City and town population statistics taken from July 1, 2007, U.S. Census Bureau estimates. Land and water area statistics taken from 2000 Census, U.S. Census Bureau.

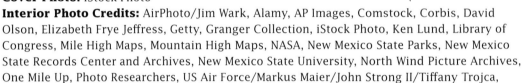

Manufactured with paper containing at least 10% post-consumer waste

Library of Congress Cataloging-in-Publication Data

Wheeler, Jill C., 1964-
  New Mexico / Jill C. Wheeler.
      p. cm. -- (The United States)
  Includes index.
  ISBN 978-1-60453-666-9
  1. New Mexico--Juvenile literature. I. Title.

  F796.3.W47 2010
  978.9--dc22
                        2008051722

Table of Contents

Land of Enchantment

Many people think of New Mexico as a bleak, barren desert. Yet, deserts can be very beautiful. In fact, artists come from all over to see the sunsets and breathtaking views of New Mexico's desert landscape. That is why the state is nicknamed the Land of Enchantment. New Mexico is also known for its many plants and animals.

New Mexico has a rich Hispanic history. It was a part of Mexico for a long time. It was also controlled by Spain for hundreds of years. This Hispanic culture makes New Mexico different from most other states.

People in New Mexico celebrate many festivals each year. The festivals honor saints, heroes, or important historical events. People from all over the state love to watch and participate in the many celebrations.

Inscription Rock, named because of the number of carvings at its base, is a beautiful part of New Mexico's El Morro National Monument.

Quick Facts

Name: The state's first explorers considered the land an addition to Mexico.

State Capital: Santa Fe, population 73,199

Date of Statehood: January 6, 1912 (47th state)

Population: 1,984,356 (36th-most populous state)

Area (Total Land and Water): 121,589 square miles (314,914 sq km), 5th-largest state

Largest City: Albuquerque, population 518,271

Nickname: Land of Enchantment

Motto: It Grows As It Goes

State Bird: Roadrunner

State Flower: Yucca

Turquoise

Piñon Pine

Wheeler Peak

WHEELER PEAK
13,161 FEET ABOVE SEA LEVEL
HIGHEST POINT IN NEW MEXICO

NAMED IN HONOR OF MAJOR GEORGE
MONTAGUE WHEELER (1832–1905) WHO
FOR TEN YEARS LED A PARTY OF
SURVEYORS AND NATURALISTS COLLECTING
GEOLOGIC, BIOLOGIC, PLANIMETRIC, AND
TOPOGRAPHIC DATA IN NEW MEXICO
AND SIX OTHER SOUTHWESTERN STATES

WHEELER PEAK WILDERNESS
Carson National Forest

Red Bluff Reservoir

State Gem: Turquoise

State Tree: Piñon Pine

State Song: "O, Fair New Mexico"

Highest Point: 13,161 feet (4,011 m), Wheeler Peak

Lowest Point: 2,842 feet (866 m), Red Bluff Reservoir

Average July Temperature: 74°F (23°C)

Record High Temperature: 122°F (50°C) near Carlsbad, June 27, 1994

Average January Temperature: 34°F (1°C)

Record Low Temperature: -50°F (-46°C) at Gavilan, February 1, 1951

Average Annual Precipitation: 14 inches (36 cm)

Number of U.S. Senators: 2

Number of U.S. Representatives: 3

U.S. Postal Service Abbreviation: NM

Geography

The square-shaped state of New Mexico is located in the southwestern United States. It is the fifth-largest state, covering 121,589 square miles (314,914 sq km). There is a lot of desert in New Mexico. There are also mountains, canyons, plateaus, and flat-topped mesas. Much of New Mexico is arid. But there is much forested land in the mountains of the northern part of the state.

There are several big rivers in New Mexico. The Rio Grande is the longest and most important. Other rivers in New Mexico include the Pecos, Canadian, San Juan, and Gila Rivers. The largest lake in New Mexico is the Elephant Butte Reservoir.

Elephant Butte Island is a rock formation created by a volcano more than 100 million years ago.

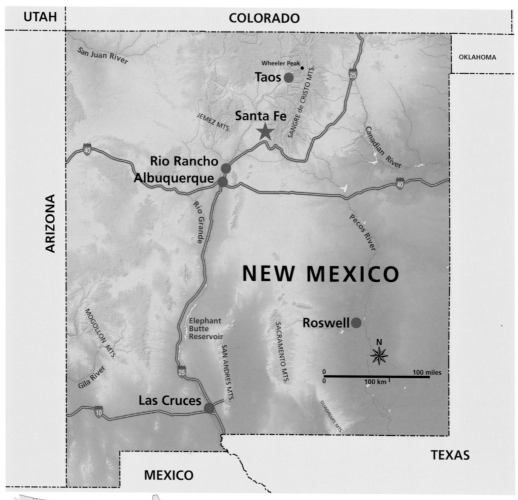

New Mexico's total land and water area is 121,589 square miles (314,914 sq km). It is the fifth-largest state. The state capital is Santa Fe.

Much of southern New Mexico is called the Basin and Range Region. Many mountain ranges are separated by extremely dry, bowl-like valleys. These valleys are called basins. The largest basin in New Mexico is the Tularosa Basin. It is located between the Organ and Sacramento Mountains.

Rocks jut up on Baldy Mountain, north of Santa Fe, New Mexico. It is in the Cimarron Range, part of the Sangre de Cristo Mountains.

New Mexico has mountains throughout its central and western regions. The Sangre de Cristo Mountains are the southernmost part of the Rocky Mountains. They are located east of the Rio Grande in northern New Mexico. The Jemez and Nacimiento Mountains are west of the river. Mountain ranges in southern New Mexico include the Mogollon, Organ, Guadalupe, Sacramento, and San Andres Mountains.

The eastern third of New Mexico features high, rolling grasslands. Cattle graze in this part of the state. The Colorado Plateau is found in the northwest part of New Mexico. There is also a 40-mile (64-km) strip of lava and craters in this part of the state. Extinct volcanoes created these craters. There are also canyons, cliffs, and mesas in the barren northwest part of New Mexico.

Shiprock is the core of an ancient volcano. It stands up from the flat, dry ground in northwestern New Mexico. It is called "Shiprock" because from a distance it looks like a sailing ship.

Climate and Weather

New Mexico is a dry state. It has mild winters and very hot summers. Southern New Mexico gets an average of less than 10 inches (25 cm) of rain per year. The mountains of northern New Mexico get an average of 20 inches (51 cm) per year. However, when it rains in New Mexico, it pours. New Mexico's dry soil sometimes cannot soak up all of the rain. Flash floods and lightning strikes are common.

New Mexico is also famous for its dust devils. Dust devils occur when the wind gathers the dry soil into twisting, funnel-shaped clouds of dirt. These clouds of dirt only occur when there has been very little rain. Dust devils are especially common in the desert.

Dust devils spin across a dry New Mexico field.

Flash floods, such as this one in Silver City, New Mexico, are common when rain comes faster than the dry soil can soak it up.

Lightning strikes over a home in New Mexico.

Plants and Animals

Three species of large predators make their home in New Mexico. These predators are black bears, cougars, and coyotes. Ranchers hate coyotes, and set traps for them. However, some coyotes are clever enough to avoid the traps and poisons. Some have also learned not to howl when they live near cities. Sometimes, people do not even know the coyotes are there.

Other common animals in New Mexico include mule deer, pronghorn antelope, squirrels, opossums, skunks, and jackrabbits.

Many kinds of snakes, lizards, turtles, and frogs are found in New Mexico. Of the 46 species of snakes, only 8 are poisonous.

The black-tailed rattlesnake's venom is poisonous.

Many cougars are found in New Mexico.

Collared Lizard

Coyote

Mule Deer

PLANTS AND ANIMALS

Forests in New Mexico make up about 21 percent of the state. These forests are home to many types of trees, including cottonwood, scrub oak, spruce, juniper, ponderosa pine, and piñon pine. Piñon pine trees are well loved in New Mexico. The smell of these trees reminds many New Mexicans of home.

The sun sets behind a saguaro cactus in the New Mexico desert.

Other plants common to New Mexico include cacti and tumbleweed. Cacti are found in deserts throughout the world. They are native to the deserts in New Mexico. Tumbleweed, however, is not native to New Mexico. It was brought to America by Ukrainian farmers. They did not know they were delivering tumbleweed. It clung to the flax seed they brought with them. Tumbleweed eventually spread throughout the western United States.

The Chama River near Abiquiu, New Mexico, wanders through fields of juniper and piñon pines mixed with grasses and trees.

New Mexico cane cholla cactus.

A tumbleweed rolls down a road.

History

The earliest settlers of New Mexico came to the area thousands of years before the first Europeans. They were from the Clovis culture, which were some of the earliest Native Americans. Later Native Americans in the area included the Anasazi culture. These early people grew corn and made pottery and woven baskets.

Anasazi is a Navajo Native American word that means "ancient ones." They built many complicated, multi-room houses, often into the sides of cliffs.

The entrance to a dwelling.

These structures are called pueblos. They helped protect the Anasazi. They could climb upwards, then pull up ladders to keep out enemies. The Anasazi eventually scattered and formed smaller groups. Eventually, other Native American groups settled in the area. These included Apache, Navajo, and Ute Indians.

The first Europeans came to New Mexico in the early 1500s. At that time, New Mexico was a remote province of Mexico, which was ruled by Spain. In 1540, Spanish explorer Francisco Vásquez de Coronado led an expedition looking for treasure. He never found the mythical Seven Golden Cities of Cibola.

In 1540, Coronado searched for treasure.

In 1610, Spanish rulers made Santa Fe the capital of New Mexico. Settlers began to move into the area. Missionaries tried to force Native Americans to change their religion and culture. In 1680, the Pueblo Rebellion pushed the Spanish out of New Mexico. But by 1692, the Spanish were back in control. The city of Albuquerque was founded in 1706.

After the Spanish returned, they gave more freedom to the Native Americans. They were allowed to practice some non-Christian traditions. Meanwhile, Spanish settlers continued to pour into the territory. They farmed, and raised sheep and horses.

In February 1821, Mexico broke away from Spain. New Mexico was still considered a part of Mexico at that time. However, New Mexico and the United States were trading goods such as wool, furs, and horses.

The Mexican-American War began in 1846. That year, General Stephen Kearny and his troops marched into New Mexico. There was little resistance. New Mexico became an official territory of the United States in 1850.

General Stephen Kearny captured Santa Fe, New Mexico, in August 1846. Four years later, New Mexico became an official United States territory.

In the late 1800s, raising cattle became an important industry for New Mexico. There was a lot of conflict between cattle and sheep farmers over who controlled the land. Also, many Navajo and Apache Native Americans rebelled against being put on reservations. Settlement continued despite the conflicts. New irrigation methods helped many farms develop.

Sheep are herded into a town.

New Mexico became the 47th state in 1912. It was still mostly an agricultural area, and isolated from the rest of the country. Automobiles and new roads changed that. People began to move from rural areas to the cities.

During World War II, many men from New Mexico joined the Army. Military research labs were based in the state. The center at Los Alamos helped create the first atomic bomb in 1945. After the war, the research centers continued their work. Military families moved to the state.

The first U.S. atom bomb test took place near Alamogordo, New Mexico, on July 16, 1945.

The state's population doubled between 1940 and 1960. Growth was helped by federal government spending on military bases, missile ranges, and science laboratories. New Mexico also became famous for its clear, healthy mountain air.

In the early 21st century, New Mexico continued to grow. Agriculture, natural gas, and mineral resources are strong industries in the state. A thriving tourism industry brings a steady stream of people to the state. Many stay and make New Mexico their new home.

Did You Know?

- The first book about any area of the United States was about New Mexico. The book was written in 1610 by Gaspar Pérez de Villagra. It was called *A History of New Mexico.*

- New Mexico was the first state to have an official state cookie. The *biscochito* was adopted as the state cookie in 1989.

- New Mexico has hundreds of ghost towns. Ghost towns are towns that have now been abandoned. There were many ghost towns in the American West after nearby gold and silver mines closed down.

- The real Smokey the Bear lived in New Mexico. The character Smokey the Bear was invented in the 1940s to teach people about forest fires. After a devastating fire in 1950, firefighters discovered a tiny black bear cub hanging in a tree. The bear was badly burned. Firefighters decided he would be called "Smokey the Bear." This real mascot helped the government's Smokey the Bear campaign get people's attention.

- People claim to have seen wreckage of an alien spaceship that crash-landed near Roswell, New Mexico, in the 1940s. Today, this town has UFO museums and many tourists. UFO stands for Unidentified Flying Objects.

People

William H. Bonney (1859-1881) was the outlaw known as Billy the Kid. His real name was Henry McCarty. He grew up in New Mexico. He was famous for gambling, stealing cattle, and being the ringleader of a gang. He escaped from prison and the death penalty twice. Legend says he killed 21 men. Finally, in 1881, he was shot dead by Sheriff Pat Garrett in the town of Fort Sumner.

Maria Martinez (1887?-1980) was a famous artist. She lived in San Ildefonso Pueblo and was a Native American. Her pottery was especially famous. She made her first piece when she was about seven years old.

John Denver (1943-1997) was a popular singer-songwriter and folksinger. He was born in Roswell, New Mexico. His songs included "Leaving on a Jet Plane," "Take Me Home, Country Roads," and "Rocky Mountain High." He died in 1997 in a plane crash.

Tony Hillerman (1925-2008) wrote many best-selling mystery novels. His stories focused on modern society and traditional Navajo customs. His most famous heroes are Joe Leaphorn and Jim Chee of the Navajo tribal police force. Hillerman was born in Oklahoma, but spent much of his life in Albuquerque, New Mexico.

Conrad Hilton (1887-1979) was born in San Antonio, New Mexico. He spent a lot of his childhood helping his father rent rooms to migrant workers. Later, he decided to buy a small hotel. Today, the Hilton chain of hotels is one of the largest hotel chains in the world.

Nancy Lopez (1957-) grew up in Roswell, New Mexico. She later became a record-breaking professional golfer. She has won 50 professional golf tournaments. She is also in the Ladies Professional Golf Association (LPGA) Hall of Fame.

Bill Mauldin (1921-2003) drew cartoons about soldiers in World War II. He showed the soldiers as they really were. His most famous characters were named Willie and Joe. Mauldin was born in 1921 in Mountain Park, New Mexico. He won two Pulitzer Prizes for his work in 1945 and 1959.

Demi Moore (1962-) is a famous Hollywood actress. She has starred in many hit movies, including *Ghost* and *A Few Good Men*. She was also the voice of Esmeralda in Disney's *The Hunchback of Notre Dame.* She was born in Roswell.

Cities

Albuquerque is the only city in New Mexico with more than 100,000 people. It has a population of 518,271. This is about one-fourth of the residents of the entire state. Albuquerque is located in the north-central part of New Mexico. The Rio Grande flows through the city. Albuquerque is one of the fastest-growing cities in America. The University of New Mexico is in Albuquerque. Many companies that produce advanced technology are here. Kirtland Air Force Base is also located in Albuquerque.

Santa Fe is the capital of New Mexico. It is located in the north-central part of the state. Santa Fe is one of the smallest state capitals in the country. It only has about 73,199 residents. Many artists come to Santa Fe. The city is known for its painters, sculptors, and authors. Music lovers enjoy the Santa Fe Opera, and the New Mexico Jazz Festival.

Taos is a small town located about 70 miles (113 km) north of Santa Fe. It has a population of 5,265 residents. This town has beautiful views of the desert and mountains. About 10 percent of the people living in Taos are artists, writers, or musicians. The city is a major Southwest tourist destination.

Las Cruces is New Mexico's second-largest city. It has a population of about 89,722 residents. The city is in the fertile Mesilla Valley, a major agricultural area thanks to irrigation. To the east of the city loom the Organ Mountains. New Mexico State University is located in Las Cruces. Nearby White Sands Missile Range also makes the defense industry important to the city.

Rio Rancho is a medium-sized city in the north-central part of New Mexico, just north of Albuquerque. Its population is 75,978. It is the third-largest city in the state. It is also the fastest growing. Intel, the maker of computer microchips, is the city's largest employer.

Roswell is a medium-sized city in southeastern New Mexico. Its population is 45,569. Cattle and horse ranches, as well as irrigation farms and dairy farms, are found in the area. Manufacturing and petroleum production are also important to the city. Roswell is most famous for being connected to the 1947 Unidentified Flying Object (UFO) incident at a nearby air base.

Transportation

More than three hundred years ago, the Camino Real Trail connected New Mexico to Mexico. This road was 1,600 miles (2,575 km) long. It was established about 1598. The trail winds through New Mexico, along the Rio Grande.

The Santa Fe Trail was another old trail. It was used to transport people and goods from Missouri to New Mexico. Today, New Mexico has approximately 61,000 miles (98,170 km) of roads and highways. Interstate I-25 follows much of the route of the old Santa Fe Trail.

The biggest airport in New Mexico is Albuquerque International Sunport. It serves about six million people each year. There are many smaller airports throughout the state, too. Railroads also serve many places in New Mexico, especially Albuquerque.

The Rio Grande Gorge Bridge is the fifth highest bridge in the United States at 650 feet (198 m). It crosses the Rio Grande River just northwest of Taos, New Mexico. It is a major east-west road and part of U.S. Route 64.

Natural Resources

About one percent of New Mexico's economy comes from farming. Farmers in New Mexico raise beef cattle, dairy cows, and sheep. They also grow hay, alfalfa, corn, wheat, sorghum, and pecans. New Mexico is also

the nation's largest commercial producer of chili peppers.

Chili peppers are grown in New Mexico.

Fourteen percent of New Mexico's economy comes from mining. About half of the mining in New Mexico is for petroleum and natural gas. The state is third in the nation in copper production. Coal is also mined. In addition, New Mexicans mine gypsum, a chalky mineral used in cements and plaster.

Two other unusual minerals mined in large quantities in New Mexico are molybdenum and potash. Molybdenum is used to manufacture steel. Potash is used in fertilizer.

An open pit molybdenum mine near Questa, New Mexico. Molybdenum is a silvery-white metal with the eighth-highest melting point of any element.

Industry

Most jobs in New Mexico involve providing services. The service industry creates jobs for salespeople, bankers, teachers, beauticians, office workers, and health care workers, plus many more.

Tourism creates thousands of jobs in New Mexico. Tourists spend approximately $5 billion each year in the state. This money helps employ people in restaurants, hotels, shops, and resorts.

The largest employer in New Mexico is the government. New Mexico's government employs people to work in state forests and monuments, as well as post offices and other government buildings.

There are also many people who work for the United States government in research labs and the military.

Three large military bases call New Mexico home. They are Kirtland Air Force Base, Holloman Air Force Base, and White Sands Missile Range.

Kirtland Air Force Base is in southeast Albuquerque. It creates more than 50,000 jobs in the area.

Holloman Air Force Base is west of Alamogordo, New Mexico. It supports more than 21,000 people.

Sports

New Mexico has no major-league professional sports teams. There are several minor league teams that play in the state. They include the Albuquerque Isotopes (baseball), the New Mexico Scorpions (hockey), and the New Mexico Wildcats (indoor football).

Fans also enjoy watching college sports, including the Lobos from the University of New Mexico, and the Aggies from New Mexico State University.

People in New Mexico enjoy outdoor activities such as skiing, hiking, and mountain biking. Fly fishing in the San Juan River and Elephant Butte Reservoir are also popular. New Mexico has many rodeos, along with horse racing.

A saddle bronc rider gets bounced high off his saddle during the New Mexico High School Rodeo in Alamogordo, New Mexico. Hundreds of people compete in rodeos across the state.

Many people come to visit and hike in the White Sands National Monument in New Mexico. The glistening white gypsum sands form large, wave-like dunes that cover 275 square miles (712 sq km) of desert.

Entertainment

Many festivals, called fiestas, take place in New Mexico. They honor saints, heroes, or historical events. There is always food, music, and friendship at New Mexico fiestas. One big fiesta held each July is the Fiestas de Taos, in the city of Taos. The weekend pageant honors a Spanish hero, Santiago de Compostela, who fought off invaders. The festival also honors Saint Anne.

The Fiestas de Santa Fe includes a huge puppet called Zozobra. He represents the sadness of the past year. He is lit on fire, which symbolizes a new year free from troubles.

Zozobra at the Fiestas de Santa Fe.

The Albuquerque International Balloon Fiesta is the world's largest hot-air balloon festival. Each October, hundreds of colorful gas and hot-air balloons fill the New Mexico skies. Hundreds of thousands of visitors come each year to the nine-day celebration.

The hot air balloons are inflated in the early morning and then go up!

Timeline

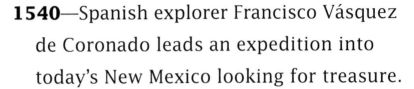

1540—Spanish explorer Francisco Vásquez de Coronado leads an expedition into today's New Mexico looking for treasure.

1610—Spanish rulers make Santa Fe the capital of New Mexico.

1680—The Pueblo Rebellion drives Spaniards out of New Mexico and Mexico.

1692-1700—Spanish forces gain back control of New Mexico.

1821—Mexico declares independence from Spain. New Mexico is no longer under Spanish rule.

1850—New Mexico becomes a territory of the United States.

1912—New Mexico becomes the 47th state.

1945—Research center at Los Alamos helps develop the first atomic bomb. The bomb is tested near Alamogordo.

1947—Rumors say that soldiers recover the remains of a UFO near Roswell.

1940-1960—New Mexico's population doubles. Massive U.S. government spending on Air Force bases, missile ranges, and science laboratories.

2000—Valles Caldera National Preserve is established.

Glossary

Anasazi—An ancient Native American culture that lived in New Mexico from around 200 BC to 1500 AD. They built their homes in the cliffs.

Basin—An area of land around a river from which water drains into the river.

Canyon—A deep, narrow river valley with steep sides.

Hispanic—Coming from, or to do with, countries where Spanish is spoken.

Irrigation—Supplying water to dry land. Rows of ditches are dug and filled with water. The water seeps into the ground, allowing plants to grow in previously unusable lands.

Mesa—A hill or mountain with steep sides and a flat top.

Migrant Workers—People who move from place to place, doing seasonal work.

Navajo—A group of Native Americans that live primarily in New Mexico, Arizona, and Utah. They are known for their work with livestock, as well as creating beautiful weavings, pottery, and silver jewelry.

Petroleum—A thick, oily liquid found below the earth's surface. It is used to make gasoline, kerosene, heating oil, and many other products.

Plateau—An area of high, flat land.

Predators—Animals that survive by eating other animals.

Pulitzer Prize—An award recognizing outstanding work in journalism, literature, or musical composition.

Reservoir—A natural or man-made area for storing a large amount of water.

Rodeo—A contest in which cowboys and cowgirls compete at riding wild horses and bulls and catching cattle with lassos.

Index